CONTENTS

One appliance, two lids, infinite possibilities

Now you have every cooking method available at your fingertips. The pressure cooker lid offers 6 wet cooking functions: use it to quickly pressure cook, sauté, steam, slow cook, sous vide and warm. The Air Fryer lid offers 5 crisp cooking functions: use it to quickly air fry, roast, bake, broil and dehydrate.

Quick, healthy, amazing

Pressure cooking and air frying both help you save time and cook healthy meals, while roasting and baking with the air fryer lid produces amazing results — without using a lot of energy or heating up your kitchen.

Guilt-free frying in your Instant Pot

Get deep-fried taste and texture with little to no oil. EvenCrisp™ technology ensures tender juicy meals with a crisp, golden finish — every time. Now you can make perfect chicken wings, crispy french fries and onion rings, battered fried vegetables and more the healthy way.

Designed for convenience and ease

Wet and dry cooking function buttons are grouped together on the control panel. Pick your cooking technique with the touch of a button. Clean up is easy too. Sleek surfaces wipe clean. And the pot, air fry basket, and broil/dehydrating tray are all dishwasher safe.

The Instant Pot Duo Cris + Air Fryer is the best of all possible worlds. With 11-in-1 functionality it does everything a regular Instant Pot does, but swap out the pressure cooker lid for the innovative air fryer lid, and you've got a whole new set of cooking techniques available — all fast, easy and at the touch of a button.

Now you have every cooking method available at your fingertips. The pressure cooker lid offers 6 wet cooking functions: use it to quickly pressure cook, sauté, steam, slow cook, sous vide and warm. The Air Fryer lid offers 5 crisp cooking functions: use it to quickly air fry, roast, bake, broil and dehydrate.

The Smart Programs make it fun and easy for anyone — from novice to chef — to prepare great healthy meals fast. And the bright displays, easy-to-use controls and easy-to-read icons that indicate cooking status make selecting programs and making adjustments simple — even during cooking. Customize the time and temperature selects for total control and save your presets so your favorite meals can be made the way you like them. And the Delay Start function ensures dinner is ready when you want it to be, and not before.

SAFTY

Instant Pot has been carefully designed to eliminate many common errors from causing harm or spoiling food. It has passed the stringent UL & ULC certification giving you uncompromised safety and peace of mind. Instant Pot protects you with 10 proven safety mechanisms and patented technologies.

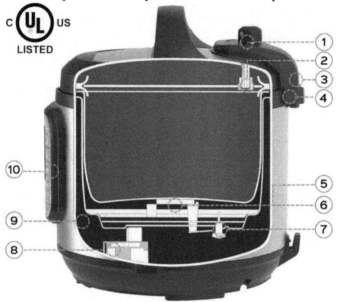

1. **Steam Release** – Releases excess pressure by venting steam through the steam release valve/handle.

2. **Anti-Block Shield** – A stainless steel cover which prevents food particles from entering the steam release pipe, reducing the risk of blockages.

3. **Safety Lid Lock** – When cooker is pressurized, the lid will automatically lock to prevent opening the cooker. Do not attempt to force the lid open while the cooker is pressurized.

4. **Lid Position Detection** – If the lid is not in a safe position for pressure cooking, the cooker will not allow cooking to begin.

5. **Automatic Temperature Control** – Regulates heating to ensure the inner pot remains within a safe temperature range, based on the program.

6. **Overheat (Burn) Protection** – Overheating may occur if:
   • After Sautéing, inner pot has not been deglazed— food is stuck to the bottom
   • The pressure cooker is being operated without sufficient cooking liquid
   • The inner pot is not making full contact with the heating element
   • The inner pot encounters a heat distribution issue, such as when starch accumulates on the bottom of the inner pot.
   The cooker will reduce the risk of burning food by lowering the heat output.

7. **Automatic Pressure Control** – Maintains working pressure levels. Suspends heating if pressure exceeds pressure level limits.

8. **Electrical Fuse** – Cuts off power if the electrical current exceeds safety limits.

9. **Thermal Fuse** – Cuts off power if the internal temperature exceeds safety limits.

10. **Leaky Lid Detection** – If there is steam leakage from the lid (such as, sealing ring not installed, or steam release handle being in "Venting" and not "Sealing" position) the cooker will not pressurize. Loss of steam may cause food to burn. The cooker monitors the pre-heating time and lowers heat output if working pressure is not reached within 40 minutes.

Care & Cleaning

The inner pot of the cooker (the stainless steel cooking pot), the sealing ring, the lid, and the steam rack are all dishwasher safe—yet another way in which your cooker makes cooking and cleanup extremely easy.

Cooker Base and Heating Element

The cooker base is home to the microprocessor and the heating element essential to cooking.

Do Not Place in the Dishwasher! If the cooker base gets wet, allow it to dry completely.

Clean the exterior of the cooker base with a damp cloth. You can use a slightly damp cloth to clean the inside of the cooker. It is however, important that the cooker be kept dry.

If you need to clean the area around the lip of the cooker, use a damp cloth or an old toothbrush to clean the edges.

Stainless Steel Inner Pot & Steam Rack

The inner pot and the steam rack are made of sturdy, food-grade stainless steel (304 – 18/8) and are entirely dishwasher safe. For the most part, you can keep the inner pot cleaned just as you would clean any stainless steel pot—by hand washing or the dishwasher.

Should the inner pot develop harmless water stains, non-abrasive scouring cleanser, made especially for cooking pots, brings back the original shine.

You can also periodically clean the inner pot by placing 1 cup of white vinegar in the bottom of the inner pot. Allow it to rest for 5 minutes, and then pour out the vinegar and rinse.

Removing Bluish Marks from Your Stainless Steel Inner Pot

Instant Pot's inner pot (cooking pot) is stainless steel, food grade 304 (18/8) with no chemical coating. It is durable and will retain its appearance for years to come with proper care.

With stainless steel cookware it is not uncommon for a bluish or "rainbow" discoloration to appear on the inside of the pot, and Instant Pot's inner pot is no exception. Minerals or salt in the food and water are the cause for this discoloration. It may be easily removed by using a non-abrasive stainless steel cleaner, which will not only remove the marks it will help to retain the original brightness.

Another option is to cover the bottom with white vinegar. Allow the vinegar to sit for 5 minutes, remove, and rinse the inner pot. The discoloration marks should be removed completely.

For "White Hard Water" stains, they can be removed with a damp sponge soaked in vinegar or lemon.

We recommend avoiding steel wool, as it will scratch the surface.

Lid

The lid is top-rack dishwasher safe. It is best to remove the sealing ring and the anti-block shield so that the lid may be thoroughly cleaned. One way to prevent the lid from retaining odors is to place it upside down on the pot until it has completely dried or you are ready to use it. Verify the steam release valve and float valve, and make sure there is no food or other debris that would block them, and prevent your cooker from coming to pressure

Anti-block Shield

The anti-block shield underneath the lid should be removed and cleaned after each use, especially following the preparation of foods that may splatter.

To remove, using your thumb, push the side of the anti-block shield towards the lid rim and lift up. It may take a little effort, but the anti-block shield should pop out.

You can now wash the shield with warm, soapy water. Rinse, wipe dry with a soft cloth, and place back in position when dry. To position the anti-block shield in place, push down.

Sealing Ring

The sealing ring is made of high-quality, heat-resistant silicone. It can be hand-washed with soapy water or placed in the dishwasher. Allow the ring to dry completely before inserting back into the lid. Ensure the sealing ring is positioned in the lid after every wash, and that it is securely in place before you start cooking.

The sealing ring is critical in the functioning of your cooker. Inspect it carefully after it is washed. Any sign of cracking or other damage, replace the sealing ring. Replace only with Genuine Instant Pot® sealing rings, using other brands may void your Instant Pot® Warranty.

As silicone may pick-up food odors during cooking you may wish to have one sealing ring for savory and another for sweet foods.

Under normal conditions it should be fine for 18 – 24 months. If you notice cracks, leaking or deformation in the sealing ring, it should be replaced immediately. However, the sealing ring is porous and may absorb odors and become discolored. To avoid discoloration and odors, you may wish to change the sealing ring every 6 – 12 months.

Condensation Collector

The condensation collector is to be removed and hand washed periodically. Allow to dry before replacing.

To Summarize

All parts of the Instant Pot with the exception of the cooker base are dishwasher safe. This includes the stainless steel inner pot, the lid, the sealing ring, and the steam rack. The cooker base must be kept dry, and can be wiped down with a damp cloth when necessary. The anti-block shield should be washed after each use and re-installed.

Sweet and Smokey Chickpeas

Cook time: 16 minutes |Serves: 4| Per serving: Calories 410; Carbs 69g; Fat 6g; Protein 20g

Ingredients:

- Chickpeas – 1 (15-ounce) can
- Aquafaba from chickpeas – 2 tbsps.
- Maple syrup – 1 tbsp.
- Smoked paprika – 2 tsps.
- Garlic powder - 1 ½ tsps.
- Sea salt – ½ tsp.

Directions:

Drain the chickpeas while reserving aquafaba obtained. Do not rinse chickpeas. Add chickpeas to the air fryer basket and shake to a single layer. Choose the air fryer function and close the lid. Air fry at 390F for 8 minutes. Meanwhile, whisk together 2 tbsps. of aquafaba, maple syrup, smoked paprika, garlic powder, and salt in a bowl. When cooked, add the chickpeas in this mixture and coat. Return the coated chickpeas with the sauce to the air fryer basket and air fryer at 390F for 5 minutes more. Shake the basket and cook again for 3 to 5 minutes. Serve.

Hot Dogs

Cook time: 8 minutes |Serves: 6| Per serving: Calories 228; Carbs 30g; Fat 8g; Protein 9g

Ingredients:

- Hot dogs – 6
- Hot dog buns - 6

Directions:

Place the hot dogs in the air fryer basket and close the lid. Cook at 400F for 4 to 6 minutes. Then remove and put them in the buns. Cook again for 2 minutes at 400F. Serve.

Mozzarella Sticks

Cook time: 8 minutes |Serves: 6| Per serving: Calories 56; Carbs 7g; Fat 1.9g; Protein 2g

Ingredients:

- Mozzarella sticks – 6 (8-ounces) each
- Panko breadcrumbs - 1 cup
- Eggs – 2
- All-purpose flour – 3 tbsps.
- Crushed black pepper – ½ tsp.
- Salt – ½ tsp.
- Marinara sauce – ¼ cup

Directions:

Freeze the mozzarella in the freezer. Beat the eggs in a bowl. Place the breadcrumbs in another bowl. Keep the all-purpose flour in another bowl. Dredge the mozzarella sticks in the flour and shake off excess. Then dip in the beaten egg and then dredge in the panko bread crumbs. Lastly, dip in the egg liquid. Line the air fryer basket with parchment and place in the mozzarella sticks. Cover and cook at 400F for 8 minutes. Serve with marinara sauce.

Sweet Potato Hash

Cook time: 15 minutes |Serves: 6| Per serving: Calories 191; Carbs 31.4g; Fat 6g; Protein 3.7g

Ingredients:

- Large sweet potato – 2, chopped
- Bacon – 2 slices
- Olive oil – 2 tbsps.
- Paprika – 1 tbsp. smoked
- Dried dill weed – 1 tsp.
- Ground black pepper – 1 tsp.
- Salt – 1 tsp.

Directions:

Preheat the air fryer at 390F for 5 minutes. In a bowl, add everything and mix. Place in the air fryer. Cook at 390F for 12 minutes. Stir the potatoes 2 to 3 times during the cooking process. Serve.

Breakfast Frittata

Cook time: 18 minutes |Serves: 2| Per serving: Calories 380; Carbs 2.9g; Fat 27.4g; Protein 31.2g

Ingredients:

- Eggs – 4, beaten
- Breakfast sausage – ¼ pound, cooked and crumbled
- Red bell pepper – 2 tbsps. chopped
- Cheddar cheese – ½ cup, grated
- Green onion – 1, chopped
- Ground cayenne pepper – ¼ tsp.
- Salt to taste and cooking spray

Directions:

In a bowl, combine the egg, sausage, grated cheddar cheese, onion, salt, and cayenne pepper. Mix well. Grease the air fryer basket with cooking spray. Pour the egg mix into the basket and cover. Close the lid and cook at 350F for 18 minutes. Serve.

Sausage Patties

Cook time: 10 minutes |Serves: 4 | Per serving: Calories 145; Carbs 0.7g; Fat 9g; Protein 14.1g

Ingredients:

- Sausage patties – 1 (12-ounce) packet
- Non-stick cooking spray

Directions:

Grease the air fryer basket and place in the patties. Do not overcrowd the basket. Spray some cooking oil on top of the patties. Cover and cook at 400F for 5 minutes. Serve.

Mac and Cheese

Cook time: 25 minutes |Serves: 6| Per serving: Calories 680; Carbs 22g; Fat 56g; Protein 22g

Ingredients:

- Macaroni - 2 ½ cups
- Sharp cheddar - 2 2/3 cups, grated
- Breadcrumbs – 1 cup
- Chicken stock - 2 cups
- Heavy cream -1 ¼ cups
- Parmesan cheese – 1/3 cup, shredded
- Butter – 8 tbsps. melted and divided
- Garlic powder – ¼ tsp.
- Salt and pepper to taste

Directions:

Place the inner pot in the Instant Pot and add the chicken broth. Add the heavy cream, four tbsps. of butter and macaroni. Pressure cook for 5 minutes or until al dente. Combine the breadcrumbs with the remaining butter in a bowl. Quick-release the pressure and stir in two cups of sharp cheddar. Top with the remaining 2/3 cup of sharp cheddar, 1/3 cup parmesan cheese and breadcrumb mixture. Air fry at 400F for 5 minutes or until browned. Serve.

Air Fried Mac and Cheese

Cook time: 35 minutes |Serves: 4| Per serving: Calories 291; Carbs 18.8g; Fat 16.5g; Protein 16.9g

Ingredients:

- Elbow macaroni – 1 cup
- Broccoli or cauliflower – ½ cup, equal size small florets
- Warmed milk – ½ cup
- Grated cheddar cheese – 1 ½ cups
- Salt and pepper
- Parmesan cheese – 1 tbsp. grated

Directions:

Preheat the air fryer at 390F. Boil some water over high heat. Lower heat and add macaroni and vegetables. Simmer for 7 to 10 minutes or until macaroni is al dente. Drain the vegetables and pasta and place them to the pot. Add cheddar cheese and milk and mix. Season with salt and pepper. Pour pasta mixture into an ovenproof dish. Then sprinkle the parmesan cheese. Bake in the air fryer basket at 350F for 15 minutes. Allow it to sit for 5 to 10 minutes in the air fryer. Serve.

Turkey Fajitas Platter

Cook time: 20 minutes |Serves: 3| Per serving: 647; Carbs 44g; Fat 39g; Protein 30g

Ingredients:

- Tortilla wraps – 6
- Leftover turkey breast – 3.5 oz.
- Avocado – 1, chopped
- Bell peppers – 3, chopped
- Small red onions – ½
- Soft cheese – 5 tbsps.
- Cajun spice – 3 tbsps.
- Mexican seasoning – 2 tbsps.
- Cumin – 1 tsp.
- Salt and pepper to taste
- Fresh coriander – ½ cup

Directions:

Slice the vegetables and chop the turkey breast into small chunks. Place everything in a bowl and mix. Place in silver foil and them place all of them in the air fryer basket. Close the lid. Cook on Air Fry more at 390F for 20 minutes. Serve.

Kale Crips

Cook time: 10 minutes |Serves: 2| Per serving: Calories 75.4; Carbs 2.3g; Fat 7g; Protein 0.8g

Ingredients:

- Kale – 1 bunch, stems and ribs removed; leaves chopped
- Olive oil – 2 tbsps.
- Salt and pepper to taste

Directions:

Preheat the air fryer to 390F. In a bowl, mix kale, olive oil, salt and pepper. Bake the kale mix in the air fryer in batches, about 5 minutes each time. Serve.

Air Fryer Carrots

Cook time: 20 minutes |Serves: 4| Per serving: Calories 126; Carbs 17g; Fat 6g; Protein 1g

Ingredients:

- Carrots – 1 lb. peeled
- Olive oil – 2 tbsps.
- Grated parmesan cheese – ¼ cup
- Salt and pepper to taste
- Garlic powder – ½ tsp.
- Paprika – ½ tsp.
- Fresh chopped parsley to taste

Directions:

In a bowl, place the carrots and toss them with oil, garlic powder, and paprika. Cook in the air fryer at 380F for 20 minutes. Shake the basket at the halfway mark. Top with parmesan cheese and parsley. Season with salt and pepper and serve.

Air Fried Quinoa

Cook time: 21 minutes |Serves: 4| Per serving: Calories 159; Carbs 27g; Fat 3g; Protein 6g

Ingredients:

- Quinoa – 2 cups, rinsed
- Water – 2 cups

Directions:

Place the rinsed quinoa in the air fryer basket and cook for 2 minutes at 320F. Then add water, mix and cook for 5 minutes at 320F. Serve.

Brussels Sprouts

Cook time: 10 minutes |Serves: 2| Per serving: Calories 72; Carbs 1.6g; Fat 7.1g; Protein 0.5g

Ingredients:

- Brussels sprouts – 2 cups, chopped
- Olive oil – 1 tbsp.
- Balsamic vinegar -1 tbsp.
- Salt – ¼ tsp.

Directions:

Mix everything in a bowl. Bake in the air fryer at 400F for 10 minutes. Shake at 5 minutes and then at 8 minutes mark. Serve.

Veggie Cake

Cook time: 12 minutes |Serves: 2| Per serving: Calories 37; Carbs 2g; Fat 3g; Protein 0.4g

Ingredients:

- Leftover vegetable bake – 1 cup
- Plain flour – 1 tbsp.

Directions:

Preheat the air fryer at 350F. Mix the flour and veggies. Make a thick dough. Grease the basket with cooking spray. Cook at 350F for 12 minutes. Flip at the halfway mark. Slice and serve.

Stuffed Garlic Mushrooms

Cook time: 25 minutes |Serves: 4| Per serving: Calories 43; Carbs 3g; Fat 3g; Protein 1g

Ingredients:

- Small mushrooms – 8
- Chopped onion – 0.7 oz.
- Breadcrumbs – 1 tbsp.
- Garlic puree – 1 tsp.
- Oil – 1 tbsp.
- Parsley – 1 tsp.
- Salt and pepper to taste

Directions:

In a bowl, mix everything except for the mushrooms. Remove the middle stalks from the mushrooms and fill the middle area with the breadcrumb mixture. Bake in the air fryer at 350F for 10 minutes. Serve.

Air-Fried Brussels Sprouts

Cook time: 16 minutes |Serves: 2| Per serving: Calories 202; Carbs 15.9g; Fat 12.32g; Protein 6.89g

Ingredients:

- Grated parmesan – 2 tbsps.
- Brussels sprouts – ½ lb. sliced
- Garlic powder – 1 tsp.
- Oil – 1 tbsp.
- Caesar dressing for dipping
- Salt and pepper to taste

Directions:

Mix everything except for the parmesan in a bowl. Coat well and cook in the air fryer at 350F for 8 minutes. Then toss and cook 8 minutes more. Garnish with parmesan and serve.

Brussels Sprout Chips

Cook time: 8 minutes |Serves: 3| Per serving: Calories 210; Carbs 12g; Fat 16.4g; Protein 6g

Ingredients:

- Brussels sprouts – ½ pound, sliced

- Garlic powder - 1 tsp.

- Olive oil – 1 tbsp.

- Parmesan – 2 tbsps. plus 2 tbsps. shredded

- Ground black pepper and salt to taste

- Caesar dressing – ¼ cup for dipping

Directions:

Toss 2 tbsps. Parmesan, sliced Brussels, and garlic powder in a bowl. Season with salt and pepper. Bake in the air fryer at 350F for 8 minutes. Shake at the halfway mark. Then remove and garnish with parmesan. Serve with Caesar dressing.

Garlic Rosemary Brussels Sprouts

Cook time: 13 minutes |Serves: 4| Per serving: Calories 154; Carbs 13g; Fat 10.6g; Protein 4g

Ingredients:

- Brussels sprouts – 1 pound, halved
- Olive oil - 3 tbsps.
- Panko breadcrumbs – ½ cup
- Garlic – 2 cloves, chopped
- Salt and pepper to taste
- Chopped fresh rosemary -1 ½ tsps.

Directions:

In a bowl, put pepper, salt, garlic, and oil and microwave for 30 seconds. Preheat the air fryer for 5 minutes at 350F. Mix the Brussels sprouts in the heated oil mixture. Cook in the air fryer for 8 minutes. Shake the basket after 5 minutes and then finish cooking. In a bowl combine breadcrumbs, remaining oil mixture and rosemary. When the cooking is over, open the air fryer and sprinkle the breadcrumb mixture over the sprouts. Close and cook for 5 minutes more. Serve.

Air Fryer Chickpeas

Cook time: 20 minutes |Serves:4 | Per serving: Calories 154; Carbs 25g; Fat 3.1g; Protein 8g

Ingredients:

- Canned chickpeas – 15 ½ ounces, rinsed and drained
- Cumin powder – ¼ tsp.
- Cayenne pepper powder – ¼ tsp.
- Salt – 1 tsp.
- Cooking spray

Directions:

Cook the chickpeas in the air fryer at 390F for 20 minutes. Meantime, combine cumin powder, cayenne pepper, and salt in a bowl. After 5 minutes, open the lid and spray some oil on the chickpeas. Sprinkle a quarter of the seasoning and stir the chickpeas with a spoon. Close and continue to cook. Shake the basket after every 5 minutes. Remove from the air fryer and add the remaining seasoning. Mix and serve.

Bang Bang Broccoli

Cook time: 20 minutes |Serves: 4| Per serving: Calories 109; Carbs 10g; Fat 5.7g; Protein 8g

Ingredients:

- Broccoli – 2 pounds, chopped
- Extra-virgin olive oil – 3 tbsps.
- Sriracha – 1 tbsp.
- Sweet chili sauce – 2 tbsps.
- Lime zest – 1
- Salt and pepper to taste

Directions:

Preheat the air fryer at 425F for 5 minutes. Whisk sriracha, chili sauce, lime zest, and oil in a bowl. Mix the broccoli with the sauce. Add salt and pepper and mix again. Cook in the air fryer for 20 minutes. Shake once. Serve.

Tofu Italian Style

Cook time: 10 minutes |Serves: 2| Per serving: Calories 342; Carbs 16g; Fat 24.4g; Protein 21g

Ingredients:

- Tofu – 8 ounces, extra-firm, drained, sliced lengthwise and excess water removed
- Broth – 1 tbsp.
- Soy sauce – 1 tbsp.
- Basil – ½ tsp. dried
- Oregano – ½ tsp. dried
- Onion powder – ½ tsp.
- Garlic powder – ½ tsp.
- Black pepper and salt to taste

Directions:

Slice the tofu into cubes and put in a Ziplock bag. Mix all the ingredients in a bowl. Add this mixture to the Ziplock bag and mix well. Preheat the air fryer at 400F for 5 minutes. Add the seasoned tofu in the air fryer and cook at 350F for 6 minutes. Open the air fryer after 4 minutes and shake the basket. Finish cooking. Serve.

Crispy Potatoes

Cook time: 18 minutes |Serves: 4| Per serving: Calories 133; Carbs 24g; Fat 3.6g; Protein 3g

Ingredients:

- Baby potatoes – 1 pound, chopped with peel
- Oil – 1 tbsp.
- Italian seasoning – 1 tsp.
- Garlic powder – 1 tsp.
- Cajun seasoning – 1 tsp.
- Salt and pepper to taste
- Lemons – 2, cut into wedges
- Chopped parsley – ¼ cup, for garnish

Directions:

Toss garlic powder, halved potatoes, Cajun seasoning, Italian seasoning, salt in a bowl and mix with potatoes. Bake in the air fryer at 400F for 18 minutes. Shake the potatoes after 10 minutes of cooking. Finish cooking and serve with lemon wedges and parsley.

Honey-Glazed Carrots

Cook time: 35 minutes |Serves: 6 | Per serving: Calories 146; Carbs 19g; Fat 8g; Protein 1g

Ingredients:

- Carrots – 2 pounds, peeled and cut lengthwise
- Honey – 2 tbsps.
- Butter – ¼ cup
- Garlic powder – ½ tsp.
- Rosemary – ½ tsp. dried
- Salt and pepper to taste
- Fresh thyme – 4 tbsps. chopped

Directions:

Melt butter in a saucepan. Add garlic powder, rosemary, honey, pepper, and salt and mix well. Remove and set aside. Add the carrots and mix. Preheat the air fryer at 400F. Line the air fryer basket with a baking sheet and cook the carrots at 400F for 35 minutes. Garnish and serve.

Bang Bang Cauliflower

Cook time: 12 minutes |Serves: 4| Per serving: Calories 100; Carbs 12g; Fat 5g; Protein 4g

Ingredients:

- Cauliflower – 21 ounces, chopped
- Olive oil – 3 tbsps.
- Garlic – 3 cloves, grated
- Lime zest of 1 lime
- Sriracha – 1 tbsp.
- Sweet chili sauce - 2 tbsps.
- Salt and pepper to taste
- Chopped cilantro – 1 tsp. for garnish

Directions:

Combine oil, chili sauce, lime juice, sriracha, and garlic in a bowl. Add the cauliflower, ground pepper, salt and mix. Cook in the air fryer at 360F for 12 minutes. Shake the basket at the halfway mark. Garnish and serve.

Crispy Chickpeas

Cook time: 20 minutes |Serves: 2| Per serving: Calories 263; Carbs 48.1g; Fat 4.8g; Protein 10.5g

Ingredients:

- Chickpeas – 1(15 oz.) can, drained and rinsed
- Olive oil – 1 tsp.
- Dry ranch seasoning mix – 1 tbsp.

Directions:

Mix oil and chickpeas in a bowl. Spread the mixture in the air fryer basket and cook at 390F for 17 minutes. Shake once at the halfway mark. Remove and toss with seasoning. Serve.

Chicken Casserole

Cook time: 15 minutes |Serves: 4| Per serving: Calories 301; Carbs 17g; Fat 17g; Protein 20g

Ingredients:

- Chicken - 3 cups, shredded
- Egg noodles – 1(12 oz.) bag (boiled in hot water for 2 to 3 minutes then drain)
- Onion – ½, chopped
- Chopped carrots – ½ cup
- Frozen peas – ¼ cup
- Frozen broccoli pieces – ¼ cup
- Celery -2 stalks, chopped
- Chicken broth – 5 cups
- Garlic powder – 1 tsp.
- Salt and pepper to taste
- Cheddar cheese – 1 cup, shredded
- French onions – 1 package
- Sour cream – ¼ cup
- Cream of chicken and mushroom soup – 1 can

Directions:

Place the chicken, vegetables, garlic powder, salt, and pepper and broth in a bowl and mix. Then place in the air fryer basket. Lightly stir the egg noodles into the mix until damp. Cook for 4 minutes at 350F. Then stir in the can of soup, sour cream, cheese and 1/3 of the French onions. Top with the remaining French onion and close. Cook for 10 minutes more. Serve.

Honey-Mustard Chicken Breasts

Cook time: 20 minutes |Serves: 6| Per serving: Calories 236; Carbs 9.8g; Fat 5g; Protein 38g

Ingredients:

- Boneless, skinless chicken breasts – 6 (6-oz, each)
- Fresh rosemary – 2 tbsps. minced
- Honey – 3 tbsps.
- Dijon mustard – 1 tbsp.
- Salt and pepper to taste

Directions:

Combine the mustard, honey, pepper, rosemary and salt in a bowl. Rub the chicken with this mixture.. Grease the air fryer basket with oil. Air fry the chicken at 350F for 20 to 24 minutes or until the chicken reaches 165F. Serve.

Air Fryer Chicken

Cook time: 30 minutes |Serves: 4| Per serving: Calories 277; Carbs 1g; Fat 8g; Protein 50g

Ingredients:

- Chicken wings – 2 lbs.
- Salt and pepper to taste
- Cooking spray

Directions:

Season the chicken wings with salt and pepper. Spray the air fryer basket with cooking spray. Add chicken wings and cook at 400F for 35 minutes. Flip 3 times during cooking for even cooking. Serve.

Chinese Duck Legs

Cook time: 36 minutes |Serves: 2| Per serving: Calories 300; Carbs 26g; Fat 12g; Protein 18g

Ingredients:

- Duck legs – 2
- Dried chilies – 2, chopped
- Olive oil – 1 tbsp.
- Star anise – 2
- Spring onions – 1 bunch, chopped
- Ginger – 4 slices
- Oyster sauce – 1 tbsp.
- Soy sauce – 1 tbsp.
- Sesame oil – 1 tsp.
- Water – 14 ounces
- Rice wine – 1 tbsp.

Directions:

Heat oil in a pan. Add water, soy sauce, oyster sauce, ginger, rice wine, sesame oil, star anise, and chili. Stir and cook for 6 minutes. Add spring onions and duck legs, toss to coat and transfer to a pan. Place the pan in the air fryer and cook at 370F for 30 minutes. Serve.

Whole Chicken

Cook time: 45 minutes |Serves: 6| Per serving: Calories 412; Carbs 1g; Fat 28g; Protein 35g

Ingredients:

- Whole chicken – 1 (2 ½ pounds) washed and pat dried
- Dry rub – 2 tbsps.
- Salt – 1 tsp.
- Cooking spray

Directions:

Preheat the air fryer at 350F. Rub the dry rub on the chicken. Then rub with salt. Cook in the air fryer at 350F for 45 minutes. After 30 minutes, flip the chicken and finish cooking. Chicken is done when it reaches 165F.

Herb Turkey Breast

Cook time: 40 minutes |Serves: 6 | Per serving: Calories 406; Carbs 1g; Fat 26.5g; Protein 42g

Ingredients:

- Turkey breast with skin – 2 pounds
- Melted butter – 4 tbsps.
- Garlic – 3 cloves, grated
- Fresh rosemary – 1 tsp. chopped
- Thyme – 1 tsp. chopped
- Ground black pepper – 1 tsp.
- Salt to taste
- Cooking spray

Directions:

Rub the turkey with salt and pepper. Combine rosemary, butter, thyme, and garlic in a bowl. Rub the turkey with this mixture. Grease the air fryer with cooking spray. Cook the turkey for 40 minutes at 375F. After 20 minutes, flip the turkey breast and spray with cooking oil. Finish cooking. Serve.

Creamy Coconut Chicken

Cook time: 25 minutes |Serves: 4| Per serving: Calories 300; Carbs 22g; Fat 4g; Protein 20g

Ingredients:

- Big chicken legs – 4
- Turmeric powder – 5 tsps.
- Ginger – 2 tbsps. grated
- Salt and black pepper to taste
- Coconut cream – 4 tbsps.

Directions:

In a bowl, mix salt, pepper, ginger, turmeric, and cream. Whisk. Add chicken pieces, coat and marinate for 2 hours. Transfer chicken to the preheated air fryer and cook at 370F for 25 minutes. Serve.

Chicken Parmesan Wings

Cook time: 15 minutes |Serves: 4| Per serving: Calories 490; Carbs 1g; Fat 22g; Protein 72g

Ingredients:

- Chicken wings – 2 lbs. cut into drumettes, pat dried
- Parmesan – ½ cup, plus 6 tbsps. grated
- Herbs de Provence – 1 tsp.
- Paprika – 1 tsp.
- Salt to taste

Directions:

Combine the parmesan, herbs, paprika, and salt in a bowl and rub the chicken with this mixture. Preheat the air fryer at 350F. Grease the basket with cooking spray. Cook for 15 minutes. Flip once at the halfway mark. Garnish with parmesan and serve.

Turkey Sausage Bake

Cook time: 30 minutes |Serves: 6| Per serving: Calories 320; Carbs 7g; Fat 20g; Protein 28g

Ingredients:

- Ground turkey sausage – 1 lb.
- Eggs - 6
- Half-and-half – ½ cup
- Cheddar cheese – ½ cup, shredded
- Broccoli – 1 small head, chopped into florets
- Red bell pepper – 1, diced
- Onion – 1, chopped
- Garlic – 2 cloves, chopped
- Olive oil – 1 tbsp.
- Salt and pepper to taste

Directions:

Heat the oil on Sauté. Sauté the sausage for 3 minutes. Add the onions and garlic and sauté for 2 minutes. Add the broccoli and red pepper and cook for 4 minutes. Then remove the mixture to a bowl. Crack the eggs in another bowl. add half-and-half, salt, and pepper then whisk to make it smooth. Grease ramekins and add about a quarter cup of the sausage mixture into each ramekin and cover with egg mixture. Sprinkle about 1 ½ tbsps. shredded cheddar cheese on top. Cook at 320F for 10 minutes. Cook in batches if necessary. Serve.

Fried Whole Chicken

Cook time: 70 minutes |Serves: 4| Per serving: Calories 436; Carbs 4g; Fat 28g; Protein 42g

Ingredients:

- Whole chicken - 1
- Oil – 2 tbsps.
- Garlic powder – 1 tsp.
- Onion powder – 1 tsp.
- Paprika – 1 tsp.
- Italian seasoning - 1 tsp.
- Steak seasoning – 2 tbsps.
- Chicken broth – 1 ½ cups

Directions:

Mix the seasoning and rub a little amount on the chicken. Pour the broth inside the air fryer basket and place the chicken. Cook for 25 minutes at 400F. Then rub the top of the chicken with oil and rub it with half of the seasoning. Cook 10 minutes more. Then flip the chicken and grease it with oil. Rub with the remaining seasoning. Cook for 10 minutes more. Rest, slice and serve.

Turkey Breasts

Cook time: 50 minutes |Serves: 4| Per serving: Calories 558; Carbs 1g; Fat 18g; Protein 98g

Ingredients:

- Boneless turkey breast – 3 lbs.
- Mayonnaise – ¼ cup
- Poultry seasoning – 2 tsps.
- Salt and pepper to taste
- Garlic powder – ½ tsp.

Directions:

Preheat the air fryer to 360F. Season the turkey with mayonnaise, seasoning, salt, garlic powder, and black pepper. Cook the turkey in the air fryer for 1 hour at 360F. Turning after every 15 minutes. The turkey is done when it reaches 165F.

BBQ Chicken Breasts

Cook time: 15 minutes |Serves: 4| Per serving: Calories 131; Carbs 2g; Fat 3g; Protein 24g

Ingredients:

- Boneless, skinless chicken breast – 4, about 6 oz. each
- BBQ seasoning – 2 tbsps.
- Cooking spray

Directions:

Rub the chicken with BBQ seasoning and marinate in the refrigerator for 45 minutes. Preheat the air fryer at 400F. Grease the basket with oil and place the chicken. Then spray oil on top. Cook for 13 to 14 minutes. Flipping at the halfway mark. Serve.

Turkey Burgers

Cook time: 25 minutes |Serves: 4| Per serving: Calories 183; Carbs 11g; Fat 3g; Protein 28g

Ingredients:

- Lean ground turkey – 1 lb.
- Unsweetened apple sauce – ¼ cup
- Chopped onion – ½
- Ranch seasoning – 1 tbsp.
- Worcestershire sauce -2 tsps.
- Minced garlic - 1 tsp.
- Plain breadcrumbs – ¼ cup
- Salt and pepper to taste

Directions:

Mix everything and make 4 patties. Keep in the refrigerator for 30 minutes. Preheat the air fryer at 360F. Grease the air fryer basket with cooking spray and place in the patties. Then spray cooking spray on top. Cook for 15 minutes. Flip at the halfway mark. Serve.

Turkey Legs

Cook time: 40 minutes |Serves: 2| Per serving: Calories 458; Carbs 3g; Fat 46g; Protein 82g

Ingredients:

- Turkey legs – 2 large, washed and pat dried
- Smoked paprika – 1 ½ tsp.
- Brown sugar – 1 tsp.
- Seasoning salt – 1 tsp.
- Garlic powder – ½ tsp.
- Oil for spraying

Directions:

Mix the paprika, sugar, salt, and garlic powder well. Rub the turkey with seasoning mixture, rub under the skin as well. Preheat the air fryer. Spray the air fryer basket with cooking spray and place the turkey legs. Then spray the turkey with oil. Cook for 400F for 20 minutes. Then flip and spray with oil. Cook 20 minutes more. Serve.

Rotisserie Chicken

Cook time: 60 minutes |Serves: 4| Per serving: Calories 534; Carbs 0g; Fat 36g; Protein 35g

Ingredients:

- Whole chicken – 1, cleaned and patted dry
- Olive oil – 2 tbsps.
- Seasoned salt – 1 tbsp.

Directions:

Remove the giblet packet from the cavity. Rub the chicken with oil and salt. Place in the air fryer basket, breast-side down. Cook at 350F for 30 minutes. Then flip and cook another 30 minutes. Chicken is done when it reaches 165F.

Lobster Tails

Cook time: 8 minutes |Serves: 2| Per serving: Calories 120; Carbs 2g; Fat 12g; Protein 1g

Ingredients:

- Lobster tails – 2 (6 oz.) butterflied
- Salt – 1 tsp.
- Chopped chives – 1 tsp.
- Unsalted butter – 2 tbsps. melted
- Minced garlic -1 tbsp.
- Lemon juice – 1 tsp.

Directions:

Combine garlic, butter, salt, chives, and lemon juice. Spread the lobster tails with butter mix and cook in the air fryer at 380F for 4 minutes. Then open and spread more butter on top. Cook for 2 to 4 minutes more. Serve.

Whitefish with Garlic and Lemon

Cook time: 10 minutes |Serves: 2| Per serving: Calories 308; Carbs 6.88g; Fat 16.47g; Protein 33g

Ingredients:

- Salt and pepper to taste
- Lemon pepper seasoning – ½ tsp.
- Whitefish fillets – 12 oz.
- Chopped parsley to taste
- Garlic powder – ½ tsp.
- Lemon wedges to taste
- Onion powder – ½ tsp.

Directions:

Coat the fish with oil. Season with onion powder, garlic powder, and lemon pepper. Then season with salt and pepper. Coat well. Line the air fryer basket with parchment and spray with oil. Arrange fish and add a few lemon wedges. Cook at 360F for 6 to 12 minutes or until fish is cooked. Flip once at the halfway mark. Serve.

Shrimps with Lemon

Cook time: 15 minutes |Serves: 2 | Per serving: Calories 117; Carbs 2g; Fat 1.66g; Protein 23.46g

Ingredients:

- Garlic powder – ¼ tsp.
- Raw shrimps -1 pound, peeled and deveined
- Oil as needed
- Chopped parsley to taste
- Black pepper and salt to taste
- Lemon wedges to serve

Directions:

In a bowl, combine shrimp with oil, salt, pepper and garlic. Mix well. Place shrimps in the air fryer basket and cook at 400F for 10 to 14 minutes. Flip the shrimp at the halfway mark. Drizzle shrimp with lemon juice and serve.

Crispy-Fried Salmon

Cook time:10 minutes |Serves: 2|Per serving: Calories 317; Carbs 10.33g; Fat 14.38g;Protein 36.66g

Ingredients:

- Thyme – ½ tsp.
- Brown sugar – 1 tsp.
- Whole grain mustard – 2 tbsps.
- Black pepper to taste
- Salmon fillets – 2 (6 oz. each)
- Olive oil – 2 tsps.
- Garlic – 1 clove, minced

Directions:

Rub the salmon with salt and pepper. In a bowl, mix the garlic, mustard, sugar, thyme, and oil. Whisk to blend. Spread the mixture on top of the salmon. Cook in the air fryer at 400F for 10 minutes. Flip once at the halfway mark. Serve.

Coconut Shrimp

Cook time: 15 minutes |Serves: 2| Per serving: Calories 406; Carbs 48.4g; Fat 9.2g; Protein 32.4g

Ingredients:

- Flour – ½ cup
- Kosher Salt – 1 tsp.
- Breadcrumbs – ¾ cup
- Shredded unsweetened coconut – ½ cup
- White pepper – ½ tsp.
- Egg whites – 2, lightly beaten
- Shrimp – 1 pound, peeled and deveined
- Sweet chili sauce to taste
- Lime zest – 2 tsps.
- Salt – 1 tsp.

Directions:

Combine flour, kosher salt, and white pepper in a bowl. Add egg whites to a second bowl. Combine breadcrumbs, coconut, lime zest, and salt in a third bowl. Dip the shrimp in the flour mixture, then in the egg mixture and lastly in the breadcrumb mixture. Coat well. Cook 12 minutes at 400F in the air fryer. Flip the shrimp after 5 minutes. Serve.

Lobster Tails with Lemon-Garlic Butter

Cook time: 10 minutes |Serves: 2| Per serving: Calories 418; Carbs 3.3g; Fat 25.8g; Protein 18g

Ingredients:

- Butter – 4 tbsps.
- Lobster tails – 2 (4-oz.) butterflied
- Lemon zest – 1 tsp.
- Chopped parsley – 1 tsp.
- Garlic – 1 clove, minced
- Lemon – 2 wedges
- Salt and black pepper to taste

Directions:

Add lobster tails in the air fryer basket with lobster meat facing upward. Add lemon zest, butter, and garlic in the Instant Pot and Sauté for 30 seconds. Then transfer 2 tbsps. of butter mixture to the small bowl and brush onto the lobster. Season lobster with salt and pepper. Place the air fryer basket in the air fryer. Cover and cook at 380F for 5 to 7 minutes. Serve lobster with melted butter, parsley and lemon wedge.

Tuna Patties

Cook time: 6 minutes |Serves: 4 | Per serving: Calories 67; Carbs 2g; Fat 1.8g;
Protein 11g

Ingredients:

- Canned tuna – 7 ounces
- Egg – 1
- Breadcrumbs – ¼ cup
- Mustard – 1 tbsp.
- Salt and pepper to taste
- Cooking spray

Directions:

Combine egg, tuna, bread crumbs, salt, pepper and mustard in a bowl. Make four patties with this mixture. Grease the air fryer basket with cooking oil. Cook the patties in Broil setting for 6 minutes. Flip the patties after 3 minutes. Serve.

Delicious Catfish

Cook time: 20 minutes |Serves: 4| Per serving: Calories 253; Carbs 26g; Fat 6g; Protein 22g

Ingredients:

- Catfish fillets – 4
- Salt and black pepper to taste
- A pinch of sweet paprika
- Parsley – 1 tbsp. chopped
- Lemon juice – 1 tbsp.
- Olive oil – 1 tbsp.

Directions:

Season catfish fillets with oil, paprika, pepper, and salt. Rub well. Cook in the air-fryer at 400F for 20 minutes. Flip the fish after 10 minutes. Divide fish on plates, drizzle lemon juice all over, sprinkle parsley and serve.

Air Fried Shrimps

Cook time: 10 minutes |Serves: 4| Per serving: Calories 122; Carbs 0.5g; Fat 4.6g; Protein 19.6g

Ingredients:

- Large shrimps - 1 lb. peeled and deveined
- Butter – 1 tbsp.
- Garlic – ½ tsp.
- Lemon juice -1 tsp.
- Parmesan cheese – 1/8 cup, grated
- Salt – 1/8 tsp.

Directions:

Remove shrimps' tails. Mix in lemon, garlic, and salt to a bowl with melted butter. Add shrimps and coat well. Line air fryer basket with parchment paper, grease with cooking spray and place in shrimps. Spray with cooking spray and cook for 8 minutes at 400F. Flip at the halfway mark and spray with cooking spray. Finish cooking and serve.

Air Fryer Salmon

Cook time: 15 minutes |Serves: 2| Per serving: Calories 202; Carbs 7g; Fat 11g; Protein 18g

Ingredients:

- Salmon fillets – 2 (6 ounces) fillets
- Olive oil – 2 tsps.
- Ground black pepper – ½ tsp.
- Mustard – 2 tbsps.
- Garlic – 1 clove, chopped
- Brown sugar -1 tbsp.
- Thyme leaves – ½ tsp.

Directions:

Rub the salmon with salt and pepper. Combine thyme, mustard, garlic, brown sugar, and oil in a bowl. Rub this mix on the salmon. Cook the salmon in the air fryer at 400F for 10 minutes. Flip at the halfway mark. Serve.

Shrimp with Bang Bang Sauce

Cook time: 24 minutes |Serves: 4| Per serving: Calories 442; Carbs 32g; Fat 23g; Protein 23g

Ingredients:

- Raw shrimp – 1 lb. peeled and deveined
- Mayonnaise – ½ cup
- Sriracha sauce – 1 tbsp.
- Sweet chili sauce – ¼ cup
- Lettuce – 1 head
- All-purpose flour – ¼ cup
- Green onions – 2 chopped
- Panko bread crumbs – 1 cup

Directions:

To make the sauce, add chili sauce, mayonnaise, and sriracha sauce in a bowl and whisk until smooth. Place flour in a bowl and panko breadcrumbs on another dish. Coat shrimp with flour then with the breadcrumbs. Line air fryer basket with parchment and grease with cooking spray. Cook shrimp for 12 minutes at 500F. Flip at the halfway mark spray cooking oil. Finish cooking. Serve with lettuce and green onions.

Baked Shrimp Scampi

Cook time: 10 minutes |Serves: 4| Per serving: Calories 422; Carbs 18g; Fat 26g; Protein 29g

Ingredients:

- Large shrimp – 1 lb.
- Butter – 8 tbsps.
- Minced garlic – 1 tbsp.
- White wine – ¼ cup
- Salt – ½ tsp.
- Cayenne pepper – ¼ tsp.
- Paprika – ¼ tsp.
- Onion powder – ½ tsp.
- Bread crumbs – ¾ cup

Directions:

Mix bread crumbs with dry seasonings in a bowl. Melt the butter on Sauté with garlic and white wine. Remove from the heat and add the shrimp and bread crumb mix. Transfer this mix to a casserole dish. Choose the Bake option and add food to the air fryer. Cook at 350F for 10 minutes. Serve.

Crumbled Fish

Cook time: 12 minutes |Serves: 4| Per serving: Calories 357; Carbs 22.5g; Fat 17.7g; Protein 26.9g

Ingredients:

- Oil – ¼ cup
- Egg – 1, beaten
- Flounder fillets – 4
- Dry bread crumbs – 1 cup
- Lemon – 1 sliced

Directions:

In a bowl, mix oil and bread crumbs. Dredge fillets into the egg, then into the bread crumbs to coat well. Cook in the air fryer at 350F for 12 minutes. Flip at the halfway mark of the cooking. Garnish with lemon slices and serve.

Marinated Salmon
Cook time: 12 minutes |Serves: 4| Per serving: Calories 267; Carbs 5g; Fat 11g; Protein 37g

Ingredients:

- Salmon – 4 fillets
- Brown sugar – 1 tbsp.
- Minced garlic – ½ tbsp.
- Soy sauce – 6 tbsps.
- Dijon mustard – ¼ cup
- Chopped green onion – 1

Directions:

In a bowl, mix mustard, soy sauce, brown sugar, and minced garlic. Pour this mixture over salmon fillets and coat well. Marinate for 30 minutes in the refrigerator. Then cook in the air fryer at 400F for 12 minutes. Garnish with green onions and serve.

Coconut Shrimp

Cook time: 9 minutes |Serves: 4| Per serving: Calories 279; Carbs 17g; Fat 11g; Protein 28g

Ingredients:

- Large raw shrimp - 1 lb. peeled and deveined with tail on
- Eggs – 2, beaten
- Panko breadcrumbs – ¼ cup
- Salt – 1 tsp.
- Black pepper to taste
- Flour – ½ cup
- Unsweetened shredded coconut – ½ cup
- Cooking spray

Directions:

Take 3 bowls. Put flour in the first, and beaten eggs in the second. Mix Breadcrumbs, coconut, salt and black pepper in the third bowl. Preheat the air fryer to 390F. Dip shrimp in flour, then in egg and then in the breadcrumb mixture. Coat well. Place in the air fryer and spray with oil. Cook in the air fryer for 4 minutes. Then flip and spray again. Cook for 5 minutes more. Serve.

Steak and Broccoli

Cook time: 12 minutes |Serves: 4| Per serving: Calories 330; Carbs 23g; Fat 12g; Protein 23g

Ingredients:

- Round steak – ¾ pound, cut into strips
- Broccoli florets – 1 pound
- Oyster sauce – 1/3 cup
- Sesame oil – 2 tsps.
- Soy sauce – 1 tsp.
- Sugar – 1 tsp.
- Sherry – 1/3 cup
- Olive oil – 1 tbsp.
- Garlic – 1 clove, minced

Directions:

In a bowl, mix sugar, sherry, soy sauce, oyster sauce, and sesame oil. Add beef, toss to coat and marinate for 30 minutes. Transfer to a bowl. Add oil, garlic, and broccoli. Toss to coat. Cook at 380F for 12 minutes. Serve.

Provencal Pork

Cook time: 15 minutes |Serves: 2| Per serving: Calories 300; Carbs 21g; Fat 8g; Protein 23g

Ingredients:

- Red onion – 1, sliced
- Yellow bell pepper – 1, cut into strips
- Green bell pepper – 1, cut into strips
- Salt and black pepper to taste
- Provencal herbs – 2 tsps.
- Mustard – ½ tsp.
- Olive oil – 1 tbsp.
- Pork tenderloin – 7 ounces

Directions:

In a dish, mix salt, pepper, onion, green bell pepper, yellow bell pepper, half the oil, and herbs and toss well. Season pork with mustard, salt, pepper, and rest of the oil. Toss well and add to veggies. Cook in the air fryer at 370F for 15 minutes. Serve.

Lamb and Brussels Sprouts

Cook time: 70 minutes |Serves: 4|Per serving: Calories 440; Carbs 2g; Fat 23g; Protein 49g

Ingredients:

- Leg of lamb – 2 pounds, scored
- Olive oil – 2 tbsps.
- Rosemary - 1 tbsp. chopped
- Lemon thyme – 1 tbsp. chopped
- Garlic – 1 clove, minced
- Brussels sprouts – 1 ½ pounds trimmed
- Butter – 1 tbsp. melted
- Sour cream – ½ cup
- Salt and black pepper to taste

Directions:

Season the leg of lamb with rosemary, thyme, salt, and pepper. Brush with oil, and place in the air fryer basket. Cook at 300F for 1 hour. Flip once at the halfway mark. Transfer to a plate and keep warm. In a pan, mix Brussels sprouts with sour cream, butter, garlic, salt, and pepper. Mix well and cook at 400F for 10 minutes. Divide lamb on plates, add Brussels sprouts on the side and serve.

Beef with Peas and Mushrooms

Cook time: 22 minutes |Serves: 2| Per serving: Calories 235; Carbs 22g; Fat 8g; Protein 24g

Ingredients:

- Beef steaks – 2, cut into strips
- Salt and black pepper to taste
- Snow peas – 7 ounces
- White mushrooms – 8 ounces, halved
- Yellow onion – 1, cut into rings
- Soy sauce – 2 tbsps.
- Olive oil – 1 tsp.

Directions:

In a bowl, mix soy sauce, and olive oil, and whisk. Add beef strips and coat. In another bowl, mix mushrooms, onion, snow peas with salt, pepper, and the oil. Toss well. Place in pan and cook in the air fryer at 350F for 16 minutes. Add beef strips to the pan as well and cook at 400F for 6 minutes more. Serve.

Lamb Shanks
Cook time: 45 minutes |Serves: 4| Per serving: Calories 283; Carbs 17g; Fat 4g; Protein 26g

Ingredients:

- Lamb shanks – 4
- Yellow onion – 1, chopped
- Olive oil – 1 tbsp.
- Coriander seeds – 4 tsps. crushed
- White flour – 2 tbsps.
- Bay leaves – 4
- Honey – 2 tsps.
- Dry sherry – 5 ounces
- Chicken stock – 2 ½ cups
- Salt and pepper to taste

Directions:

Season the lamb shanks with salt and pepper. Rub with half of the oil and cook in the air fryer at 360F for 10 minutes. Heat up a pan that fits in the air fryer with the rest of the oil over medium-high heat. Add onion and coriander. Stir and cook for 5 minutes. Add salt, pepper, bay leaves, honey, stock, sherry, and flour. Stir, bring to a simmer, and add the lamb. Mix well. Cook in the air fryer at 360F for 30 minutes. Serve.

Chorizo and Beef Burger

Cook time: 15 minutes |Serves: 4| Per serving: Calories 291; Carbs 3.8g; Fat 18.3g; Protein 21.6g

Ingredients:

- 80/20 ground beef – ¾ pound
- Ground chorizo – ¼ pound
- Chopped onion – ¼ cup
- Pickled jalapenos – 5 slices, chopped
- Chili powder – 2 tsps.
- Minced garlic -1 tsp.
- Cumin – ¼ tsp.

Directions:

Mix all the ingredients in a bowl. Make four burger patties from the mixture. Place burger patties into the air fryer basket. Cook at 375F for 15 minutes. Flip once. Serve.

Lamb with Potatoes

Cook time: 45 minutes |Serves: 6| Per serving: Calories 273; Carbs 25g; Fat 4g; Protein 29g

Ingredients:

- Lamb roast – 4 pounds
- Rosemary – 1 spring
- Garlic – 3 cloves, minced
- Potatoes – 6, halved
- Lamb stock – ½ cup
- Bay leaves – 4
- Salt and pepper to taste

Directions:

Put potatoes in a dish. Add salt, pepper, rosemary spring, garlic, bay leaves, stock, and lamb. Mix and place in the air fryer. Cook at 360F for 45 minutes. Slice lamb, divide among plates, and serve with potatoes and cooking juices.

Beef with Mayo

Cook time: 40 minutes |Serves: 8| Per serving: Calories 400; Carbs 27g; Fat 12g; Protein 19g

Ingredients:

- Mayonnaise – 1 cup
- Sour cream – 1/3 cup
- Garlic – 3 cloves, minced
- Beef fillet – 3 pounds
- Chives – 2 tbsps. chopped
- Mustard – 2 tbsps.
- Tarragon – ¼ cup, chopped
- Salt and black pepper to taste

Directions:

Season beef with salt and pepper and place in the air fryer. Cook at 370F for 20 minutes. Transfer to a plate and set aside. In a bowl, mix garlic with salt, pepper, mayo, chives, and sour cream. Whisk and set aside. In another bowl, mix mustard with tarragon, and Dijon mustard. Whisk, and add beef. Mix well. Return to the air fryer and cook at 350F for 20 minutes more. Divide beef on plates, spread garlic mayo on top and serve.

Italian Stuffed Bell Peppers

Cook time: 25 minutes |Serves: 4| Per serving: Calories 358; Carbs 8.7g; Fat 24.1g; Protein 21.1g

Ingredients:

- Ground pork Italian sausage – 1 pound
- Garlic powder – ½ tsp.
- Dried parsley – ½ tsp.
- Diced Roma tomato – 1
- Chopped onion – ¼ cup
- Green bell pepper – 4
- Shredded mozzarella cheese – 1 cup, divided

Directions:

Brown the ground sausage on Sauté in the Instant Pot until no longer pink. Drain fat. Add the onion, tomato, parsley, and garlic powder. Cook for 3 to 5 minutes more. Slice peppers in half and remove the seeds and white membrane. Spoon the meat mixture evenly into pepper halves. Top with mozzarella and place pepper halves into the air fryer basket. Cook at 350F for 15 minutes. Serve.

Bacon Casserole

Cook time: 20 minutes |Serves: 4| Per serving: Calories 369; Carbs 1g; Fat 22.6g; Protein 31g

Ingredients:

- 80/20 ground beef – 1 pound
- White onion – ¼, chopped
- Shredded cheddar cheese – 1 cup, divided
- Egg – 1
- Bacon – 4 slices, cooked and crumbled
- Pickle spears – 2, chopped

Directions:

Brown the ground beef in the Instant Pot on Sauté for 7 to 10 minutes. Drain the fat. Add the ground beef to a bowl. Add egg, ½-cup cheddar and onion to the bowl. Mix well and add crumbled bacon. Pour the mixture into a round baking dish and top with remaining cheddar. Place into the air fryer basket. Cook at 375F for 20 minutes. Serve topped with chopped pickles.

Marinated Beef

Cook time: 45 minutes |Serves: 6| Per serving: Calories 500; Carbs 29g; Fat 9g; Protein 36g

Ingredients:

- Bacon strips – 6
- Butter – 2 tbsps.
- Garlic – 3 cloves, minced
- Salt and black pepper to taste
- Horseradish – 1 tbsp.
- Mustard – 1 tbsp.
- Beef roast – 3 pounds
- Beef stock – 1 ¾ cups
- Red wine – ¾ cup

Directions:

In a bowl, mix butter with horseradish, salt, pepper, garlic, and mustard. Whisk and rub the beef with this mix. Arrange bacon strips on a cutting board. Place beef on top and fold bacon around beef. Place in the air fryer basket and cook at 400F for 15 minutes and transfer to a pan. Add stock and wine to the beef. Place the pan in the air fryer and cook at 360F for 30 minutes. Carve beef, divide among plates, and serve.

Beef and Green Onions

Cook time: 20 minutes |Serves: 4| Per serving: Calories 329; Carbs 26g; Fat 8g; Protein 22g

Ingredients:

- Green onion - 1 cup, chopped
- Soy sauce – 1 cup
- Water – ½ cup
- Brown sugar – ¼ cup
- Sesame seeds – ¼ cup
- Garlic – 5 cloves, minced
- Black pepper – 1 tsp.
- Lean beef – 1 pound

Directions:

In a bowl, mix the onion with water, soy sauce, garlic, sugar, sesame seeds, and pepper. Whisk and add meat. Marinate for 10 minutes. Drain beef. Cook in the preheated 390F air fryer for 20 minutes. Serve.

Creamy Pork

Cook time: 22 minutes |Serves: 6| Per serving: Calories 300; Carbs 26g; Fat 4g; Protein 34g

Ingredients:

- Pork meat – 2 pounds, boneless and cubed
- Yellow onions – 2, chopped
- Olive oil – 1 tbsp.
- Garlic – 1 clove, minced
- Chicken stock – 3 cups
- Sweet paprika – 2 tbsps.
- Salt and black pepper to taste
- White flour – 2 tbsps.
- Sour cream – 1 ½ cups
- Dill – 2 tbsps. chopped

Directions:

In a pan, mix pork with oil, salt, and pepper. Mix and place in the air fryer. Cook at 360F for 7 minutes. Add the sour cream, dill, flour, paprika, stock, garlic, and onion and mix. Cook at 370F for 15 minutes more. Serve.

Lamb Chops

Cook time: 10 minutes |Serves: 4| Per serving: Calories 231; Carbs 14g; Fat 7g; Protein 23g

Ingredients:

- Olive oil – 3 tbsps.
- Lamb chops – 8
- Salt and black pepper to taste
- Garlic – 4 cloves, minced
- Oregano – 1 tbsp. chopped
- Coriander – 1 tbsp. chopped

Directions:

In a bowl, mix oregano with garlic, oil, salt, pepper, and lamb chops and coat well. Cook in the air fryer at 400F for 10 minutes. Serve.

Crispy Lamb

Cook time: 30 minutes |Serves: 4| Per serving: Calories 230; Carbs 10g; Fat 2g; Protein 12g

Ingredients:

- Bread crumbs – 1 tbsp.
- Macadamia nuts – 2 tbsps. toasted and crushed
- Olive oil – 1 tbsp.
- Garlic – 1 clove, minced
- Rack of lamb – 28 ounces
- Salt and black pepper to taste
- Egg – 1
- Rosemary – 1 tbsp. chopped

Directions:

Mix oil, and garlic in a bowl and stir well. Season lamb with salt, pepper, and brush with oil. In another bowl, mix nuts with rosemary and breadcrumbs. Put the egg in a separate bowl and whisk well. Dip lamb in egg, then in the macadamia mix, place them in your air fryer's basket. Cook at 360F for 25 minutes. Then increase heat to 400F and cook for 5 minutes more. Serve.

Apple Snack
Cook time: 5 minutes |Serves: 4| Per serving: Calories 200; Carbs 20g; Fat 4g; Protein 3g

Ingredients:

- Big apples – 3, cored, peeled and cubed
- Lemon juice – 2 tsps.
- Pecans – ¼ cup, chopped
- Dark chocolate chips – ½ cup
- Clean caramel sauce – ½ cup

Directions:

Mix apples and lemon juice in a bowl. Add to a dish that fits in the air fryer. Add pecans, chocolate chips, and drizzle the caramel sauce. Toss to coat. Cook at 320F for 5 minutes in the air fryer. Serve.

Pesto Crackers

Cook time: 17 minutes |Serves: 6| Per serving: Calories 200; Carbs 4g; Fat 20g; Protein 7g

Ingredients:

- Baking powder – ½ tsp.
- Salt and black pepper to taste
- Flour – 1 ¼ cups
- Basil – ¼ tsp. dried
- Garlic – 1 clove, minced
- Basil pesto - 2 tbsps.
- Butter – 3 tbsps.

Directions:

Mix butter, pesto, basil, cayenne, garlic, flour, baking powder, salt, and pepper in a bowl and make a dough. Spread the dough on a lined baking sheet. Bake in the air fryer at 325F for 17 minutes. Cool and cut into crackers. Serve.

Coconut Chicken Bites

Cook time: 13 minutes |Serves: 4| Per serving: Calories 252; Carbs 14g; Fat 4g; Protein 24g

Ingredients:

- Garlic powder – 2 tsps.
- Eggs – 2
- Salt and black pepper to taste
- Panko bread crumbs – ¾ cup
- Coconut – ¾ cup, shredded
- Cooking spray
- Chicken tenders – 8

Directions:

Mix eggs with garlic powder, salt, and pepper in a bowl and whisk well. In another bowl, mix coconut with panko and stir well. Dip chicken tenders in the eggs mix and then coat in coconut thoroughly. Spray chicken bits with cooking spray. Place them in the air fryer basket and cook them at 350F for 10 minutes. Serve.

Zucchini Chips

Cook time: 1 hour |Serves: 6| Per serving: Calories 40; Carbs 3g; Fat 3g; Protein 7g

Ingredients:

- Zucchinis – 3, thinly sliced
- Salt and black pepper to taste
- Olive oil – 2 tbsps.
- Balsamic vinegar – 2 tbsps.

Directions:

Mix vinegar, oil, salt, and pepper and whisk well. Add zucchini slices and toss to coat. Cook in the air fryer at 200F for 1 hour. Shake once. Serve.

Crab Sticks
Cook time: 12 minutes |Serves: 4| Per serving: Calories 110; Carbs 4g; Fat 0g;
Protein 2g

Ingredients:

- Crabsticks – 10, halved
- Sesame oil – 2 tsps.
- Cajun seasoning – 2 tsps.

Directions:

Put crab sticks in a bowl. Add seasoning and sesame oil. Toss and place in the air fryer basket. Cook at 350F for 12 minutes. Serve.

Garlic Parmesan Chicken Wings
Cook time: 25 minutes |Serves: 4| Per serving: Calories 356; Carbs 2.1g; Fat 42.1g;
Protein 41.8g

Ingredients:

- Raw chicken wings – 2 pounds
- Salt – 1 tsp.
- Garlic powder – ½ tsp.
- Baking powder – 1 tbsp.
- Unsalted butter – 4 tbsps. melted
- Grated Parmesan cheese – 1/3 cup
- Dried parsley – ¼ tsp.

Directions:

Place chicken wings, salt, ½ tsp. garlic powder, and baking powder in a bowl. Coat and place wings into the air fryer basket. Cook at 400F for 25 minutes. Toss the basket two or 3 times during the cooking time. Combine butter, parmesan, and parsley in a bowl. Remove wings from the air fryer and place into a bowl. Pour the butter mixture over the wings and toss to coat. Serve warm.

Pork Rind Tortillas

Cook time: 5 minutes |Serves: 4| Per serving: Calories 145; Carbs 1g; Fat 10g; Protein 10.7g

Ingredients:

- Pork rinds – 1 ounce, ground
- Shredded mozzarella cheese – ¾ cup
- Full-fat cream cheese – 2 tbsps. chopped
- Egg – 1

Directions:

Place mozzarella into a bowl. Add cream cheese then to the bowl. Microwave for 30 seconds, or until both types of cheese are melted. Add the egg and ground pork rinds to the cheese mixture. Stir and make a ball. Separate the dough into four small balls. Place each ball of dough between two sheets of parchment and roll into a ¼ flat layer. Place tortillas into the air fryer basket in a single layer. Set the temperature to 400F and cook for 5 minutes. Serve.

Mozzarella Sticks

Cook time: 10 minutes |Serves: 3| Per serving: Calories 236; Carbs 4.7g; Fat 13.8g; Protein 19.2g

Ingredients:

- Mozzarella string cheese sticks – 6 (1-ounce)
- Grated Parmesan cheese – ½ cup
- Pork rinds – ½ ounce, finely ground
- Dried parsley – 1 tsp.
- Eggs – 2

Directions:

Cut the mozzarella sticks in half. Freeze until firm. In a bowl, mix ground pork rinds, Parmesan, and parsley. Whisk eggs in another bowl. Dip a frozen mozzarella stick into beaten eggs and then into the Parmesan mixture to coat. Repeat with the remaining sticks. Place mozzarella stick into the air fryer basket. Cook at 400F for 10 minutes or until golden. Serve warm.

Buffalo Chicken Dip

Cook time: 10 minutes |Serves: 4| Per serving: Calories 472; Carbs 6g; Fat 32g; Protein 25g

Ingredients:

- Cooked chicken breast – 1 cup, diced
- Full-fat cream cheese – 8 ounces, softened
- Buffalo sauce – ½ cup
- Full-fat ranch dressing – 1/3 cup
- Chopped pickled jalapenos – 1/3 cup
- Shred cheddar cheese – 1 ½ cups, divided
- Scallions – 2, sliced

Directions:

Place chicken into a large bowl. Add buffalo sauce, cream cheese, and ranch dressing. Stir to mix well. Fold in jalapenos and 1-cup cheddar. Pour the mixture into a round baking dish and place remaining cheddar on top. Place dish into the air fryer basket. Cook at 350F for 10 minutes. Top with sliced scallions and serve warm.

Cheese Bread

Cook time: 15 minutes |Serves: 4| Per serving: Calories 273; Carbs 2g; Fat 18g; Protein 20g

Ingredients:

- Shredded mozzarella cheese – 2 cups
- Grated parmesan cheese – ¼ cup
- Chopped pickled jalapenos – ¼ cup
- Eggs – 2
- Bacon – 4 slices, cooked and chopped

Directions:

Mix all ingredients in a bowl. Cover the air fryer basket with parchment paper. Press out the mixture into a circle with damp hands. Or you can make two smaller circles. Place the cheese bread into the air fryer basket. Cook at 320F for 15 minutes. Flip the bread with 5 minutes remaining. The bread should be golden brown when fully cooked. Serve warm.

Chickpeas Snack

Cook time: 10 minutes |Serves: 4| Per serving: Calories 140; Carbs 20g; Fat 1g; Protein 6g

Ingredients:

- Canned chickpeas – 15 ounces, drained
- Cumin – ½ tsp. ground
- Olive oil – 1 tbsp.
- Smoked paprika – 1 tsp.
- Salt and black pepper to taste

Directions:

In a bowl, mix chickpeas with oil, salt, pepper, paprika, and cumin. Toss to coat and place in the air fryer basket. Cook at 390F for 10 minutes. Serve.

Prosciutto-Parmesan Asparagus

Cook time: 10 minutes |Serves: 4| Per serving: Calories 263; Carbs 4.3g; Fat 20.2g; Protein 13.9g

Ingredients:

- Asparagus – 1 pound
- Prosciutto – 12 (0.5 ounce) slices
- Coconut oil – 1 tbsp. melted
- Lemon juice – 2 tsps.
- Red pepper flakes – 1/8 tsp.
- Grated Parmesan cheese – 1/3 cup
- Salted butter – 2 tbsps. melted

Directions:

On a clean work surface, place a few asparagus spears onto a sliced of prosciutto. Drizzle with lemon juice and coconut oil. Sprinkle Parmesan and red pepper flakes across asparagus. Roll prosciutto around asparagus spears. Place into the air fryer basket. Repeat. Cook at 375F and 10 minutes. Drizzle the asparagus rolls with butter before serving.

Banana Chips

Cook time: 15 minutes |Serves: 4| Per serving: Calories 121; Carbs 3g; Fat 1g; Protein 3g

Ingredients:

- Bananas – 4, peeled and sliced
- Salt – 1 pinch
- Turmeric powder – ½ tsp.
- Chaat masala – ½ tsp.
- Olive oil – 1 tsp.

Directions:

In a bowl, mix banana slices with oil, chaat masala, turmeric, and salt. Toss and set aside for 10 minutes. Cook in the air fryer at 360F for 15 minutes. Flipping them once. Serve.

Beef Jerky

Cook time: 1 hour 30 minutes |Serves: 6| Per serving: Calories 300; Carbs 3g; Fat 12g; Protein 8g

Ingredients:

- Soy sauce – 2 cups
- Worcestershire sauce – ½ cup
- Black peppercorns – 2 tbsps.
- Black pepper – 2 tbsps.
- Beef round – 2 pounds, sliced

Directions:

In a bowl, mix Worcestershire sauce, black pepper, black peppercorns, and soy sauce and whisk well. Add beef slices. Coat and keep in the refrigerator for 6 hours to marinate. Cook in the air-fryer at 370F for 1 hour and 30 minutes. Transfer to a bowl and serve.

Buffalo Cauliflower Snack

Cook time: 15 minutes |Serves: 4| Per serving: Calories 241; Carbs 8g; Fat 4g; Protein 4g

Ingredients:

- Cauliflower florets – 4 cups
- Panko bread crumbs – 1 cup
- Butter – ¼ cup, melted
- Buffalo sauce – ¼ cup
- Mayonnaise for serving

Directions:

In a bowl, mix butter and buffalo sauce and whisk well. Dip cauliflower florets in the mix and coat them in panko bread crumbs. Place them in the air fryer's basket and cook at 350F for 15 minutes. Serve.

Cheesecake

Cook time: 15 minutes |Serves: 15 | Per serving: Calories 245; Carbs 20g; Fat 12g; Protein 3g

Ingredients:

- Cream cheese – 1 pound
- Vanilla extract – ½ tsp.
- Eggs – 2
- Sugar – 4 tbsps.
- Graham crackers – 1 cup, crumbled
- Butter – 2 tbsps.

Directions:

Mix crackers with the butter in a bowl. Press crackers mix on the bottom of a lined cake pan. Place in the air fryer and cook at 350F for 4 minutes. Meanwhile, in a bowl, mix eggs, cream cheese, sugar, and vanilla and whisk well. Spread filling over crackers crust and cook in the air fryer at 310F for 15 minutes. Cool and keep in the refrigerator for 3 hours. Slice and serve.

Apple Bread

Cook time: 40 minutes |Serves: 6| Per serving: Calories 192; Carbs 14g; Fat 6g; Protein 7g

Ingredients:

- Apples – 3, cored and cubed
- Sugar – 1 cup
- Vanilla – 1 tbsp.
- Eggs – 2
- Apple pie spice – 1 tbsp.
- White flour – 2 cups
- Baking powder – 1 tbsp.
- Butter – 1 stick
- Water – 1 cup

Directions:

In a bowl, mix 1 stick butter, eggs, apple pie spice, and sugar and stir with a mixer. Add apples and stir well. In another bowl, mix flour and baking powder. Combine the 2 mixtures. Stir and pour into a springform pan. Put springform pan in the air fryer and cook at 320F for 40 minutes. Slice and serve.

Ginger Cheesecake

Cook time: 20 minutes |Serves: 6| Per serving: Calories 412; Carbs 20g; Fat 12g; Protein 6g

Ingredients:

- Butter – 2 tsps. melted
- Ginger cookies – ½ cup, crumbled
- Cream cheese – 16 ounces, soft
- Eggs – 2
- Sugar – ½ cup
- Rum – 1 tsp.
- Vanilla extract – ½ tsp.
- Nutmeg – ½ tsp. ground

Directions:

Grease a pan with butter and spread cookie crumbs on the bottom. In a bowl, beat cream cheese, eggs, rum, vanilla, and nutmeg. Whisk well and spread over the cookie crumbs. Place in the air fryer and cook at 340F for 20 minutes. Cool and keep in the refrigerator. Slice and serve.

Special Brownies

Cook time: 17 minutes |Serves: 4| Per serving: Calories 223; Carbs 3g; Fat 32g; Protein 6g

Ingredients:

- Egg – 1
- Cocoa powder – 1/3 cup
- Sugar – 1/3 cup
- Butter – 7 tbsps.
- Vanilla extract – ½ tsp.
- White flour – ¼ cup
- Walnuts – ¼ cup, chopped
- Baking powder – ½ tsp.
- Peanut butter – 1 tbsp.

Directions:

Add 6 tbsps. butter and sugar in a pan and heat over medium heat. Stir and cook for 5 minutes. Transfer to a bowl. Add flour, walnuts, baking powder, egg, cocoa powder, vanilla extract, and salt. Mix well and pour into a pan. In a bowl, mix peanut butter and 1 tbsp. butter. Heat up in the microwave for a few seconds. Mix well and drizzle over brownie mix. Place the pan in the air fryer and bake at 320F for 17 minutes. Cool, cut and serve.

Almond Butter Cookie Balls

Cook time: 10 minutes |Serves: 10| Per serving: Calories 224; Carbs 1.3g; Fat 16g; Protein 11.2g

Ingredients:

- Almond butter – 1 cup
- Egg - 1
- Vanilla extract – 1 tsp.
- Low carb protein powder – ¼ cup
- Powdered erythritol – ¼ cup
- Unsweetened coconut – ¼ cup, shredded
- Chocolate chips – ¼ cup
- Ground cinnamon – ½ tsp.

Directions:

Mix egg and almond butter in a bowl. Add erythritol, protein powder, and vanilla. Fold in cinnamon, chocolate chips, and coconut. Roll into 1-inch balls. Place balls into a baking pan and put into the air fryer basket. Cook at 320F for 10 minutes. Cool and serve.

Peanut Butter Cookies

Cook time: 8 minutes |Serves: 8 | Per serving: Calories 210; Carbs 2.1g; Fat 17.5g; Protein 8.8g

Ingredients:

- Smooth peanut butter – 1 cup
- Granular erythritol – 1/3 cup
- Egg – 1
- Vanilla extract – 1 tsp.

Directions:

Mix all the ingredients in a bowl until smooth. Continue to stir until the mixture begins to thicken. Roll the mixture into eight balls and press gently down to flatten into 2-inch round disks. Line the air fryer basket with parchment. Place the cookies onto the parchment. Work in batches if necessary. Cook at 320F for 8 minutes. Flip the cookies at the 6-minute mark. Serve.

Pecan Brownies

Cook time: 20 minutes |Serves: 6| Per serving: Calories 215; Carbs 2.3g; Fat 18.9g; Protein 4.2g

Ingredients:

- Almond flour – ½ cup
- Powdered erythritol – ½ cup
- Unsweetened cocoa powder – 2 tbsps.
- Baking powder – ½ tsp.
- Unsalted butter – ¼ cup, softened
- Egg – 1
- Chopped pecans – ¼ cup
- Chocolate chips – ¼ cup

Directions:

Mix almond flour, baking powder, cocoa powder, and erythritol in a bowl. Stir in egg and butter. Fold in chocolate chips and pecans. Scoop mixture into a baking pan and place the pan into the air fryer basket. Cook at 300F for 20 minutes. Cool, sliced and serve.

Chocolate Mayo Cake

Cook time: 25 minutes |Serves: 6| Per serving: Calories 270; Carbs 3g; Fat 25g; Protein 7g

Ingredients:

- Almond flour – 1 cup
- Salted butter – ¼ cup, melted
- Granular erythritol – ½ cup, plus 1 tbsp.
- Vanilla extract – 1 tsp.
- Full-fat mayonnaise – ¼ cup
- Unsweetened cocoa powder – ¼ cup
- Eggs – 2

Directions:

Mix all the ingredients in a bowl until smooth. Pour batter into a round baking pan. Place the pan into the air fryer basket. Cook at 300F for 25 minutes. Cool and serve.

Molten Lava Cakes

Cook time: 12 minutes |Serves: 4| Per serving: Calories 360; Carbs 19g; Fat 29g; Protein 5.2g

Ingredients:

- Self-raising flour – 1.5 tbsps.
- Baker's sugar – 3.5 tbsps.
- Unsalted butter – 3.5 oz.
- Dark chocolate – 3.5 oz. chopped
- Eggs – 2

Directions:

Preheat the air fryer to 375F. Grease and flour 4 ramekins. Melt butter and dark chocolate in the microwave. Stirring throughout. Mix sugar and egg until frothy and pale. Pour melted chocolate mixture into the egg mixture. Stir in flour and mix everything. Fill the ramekins about ¾ full with batter. Bake in the air fryer at 375F for 10 minutes. Remove, cool and serve.

Mini Cheesecake

Cook time: 15 minutes |Serves: 2| Per serving: Calories 531; Carbs 5.1g; Fat 48.3g; Protein 11.4g

Ingredients:

- Walnuts – ½ cup
- Salted butter – 2 tbsps.
- Granular erythritol – 2 tbsps.
- Full-fat cream cheese – 4 ounces, softened
- Egg – 1
- Vanilla extract – ½ tsp.
- Powdered erythritol – 1/8 cup

Directions:

Place granular erythritol, butter, and walnuts in a food processor. Pulse until a dough forms. Press dough into a 4-inch springform pan and place the pan into the air fryer basket. Cook at 400F for 5 minutes. Remove, and cool. In a bowl, mix egg, cream cheese, powdered erythritol, and vanilla extract until smooth. Spoon mixture on top of baked walnut crust and place into the air fryer basket. Cook at 300F for 10 minutes. Chill for 2 hours and serve.

Mini Chocolate Chip Pan Cookie

Cook time: 7 minutes |Serves: 4| Per serving: Calories 188; Carbs 2.3g; Fat 15.7g; Protein 5.6g

Ingredients:

- Almond flour – ½ cup
- Powdered erythritol – ¼ cup
- Unsalted butter – 2 tbsps. softened
- Egg – 1
- Unflavored gelatin – ½ tsp.
- Baking powder – ½ tsp.
- Vanilla extract – ½ tsp.
- Chocolate chips – 2 tbsps.

Directions:

Mix almond and erythritol in a bowl. Stir in gelatin, egg, and butter. Mix until combined. Stir in vanilla and baking powder and then fold in chocolate chips. Pour batter into a round baking pan and place the pan into the air fryer basket. Cook at 300F for 7 minutes. Cool and serve.

Brownies

Cook time: 20 minutes |Serves: 6| Per serving: Calories 215; Carbs 2.3g; Fat 18.9g; Protein 4.2g

Ingredients:

- Almond flour – ½ cup
- Powdered erythritol – ½ cup
- Unsweetened cocoa powder – 2 tbsps.
- Baking powder – ½ tsp.
- Unsalted butter – ¼ cup, softened
- Egg – 1
- Chopped pecans – ¼ cup
- Chocolate chips – ¼ cup

Directions:

Mix almond flour, baking powder, cocoa powder, and erythritol in a bowl. Stir in egg and butter. Fold in chocolate chips and pecans. Scoop mixture into a baking pan and place the pan into the air fryer basket. Cook at 300F for 20 minutes. Cool, slice and serve.

Mini Lava Cakes

Cook time: 20 minutes |Serves: 3| Per serving: Calories 201; Carbs 23g; Fat 7g; Protein 4g

Ingredients:

- Egg – 1
- Sugar – 4 tbsps.
- Olive oil – 2 tbsps.
- Milk – 4 tbsps.
- Flour – 4 tbsps.
- Cocoa powder – 1 tbsp.
- Baking powder – ½ tsp.
- Orange zest – ½ tsp.

Directions:

In a bowl, mix oil, sugar, milk, egg, flour, salt, cocoa powder, baking powder, and orange zest. Mix well and pour into greased ramekins. Add ramekins to the air fryer and cook at 320F for 20 minutes. Serve.

Cocoa Cake

Cook time: 17 minutes |Serves: 6 | Per serving: Calories 340; Carbs 25g; Fat 11g; Protein 5g

Ingredients:

- Butter – 3.5 ounces, melted
- Eggs – 3
- Sugar – 3 ounces
- Cocoa powder – 1 tsp.
- Flour – 3 ounces
- Lemon juice – ½ tsp.

Directions:

In a bowl, mix cocoa powder, with 1 tbsp. butter and whisk. In another bowl, mix the rest of the butter with lemon juice, flour, eggs, and sugar. Whisk well and pour half into a cake pan. Add half of the cocoa mix, spread, add the rest of the butter layer and top with the rest of the cocoa. Cook in the air fryer at 360F for 17 minutes. Cool, sliced and serve.

Bread Pudding

Cook time: 1 hour |Serves: 4| Per serving: Calories 302; Carbs 23g; Fat 8g; Protein 10g

Ingredients:

- Glazed doughnuts – 6, crumbled
- Cherries – 1 cup
- Egg – 4 yolks
- Whipping cream – 1 ½ cups
- Raisins – ½ cup
- Sugar – ¼ cup
- Chocolate chips – ½ cup

Directions:

In a bowl, mix cherries, with egg yolks, and whipping cream and stir well. In another bowl, mix doughnuts, chocolate chips, sugar, and raisins. Mix. Combine 2 mixtures and transfer everything to a greased pan that fits in your air fryer and cook at 310F for 1 hour. Chill pudding before cutting and serve.

CPSIA information can be obtained
at www.ICGtesting.com
Printed in the USA
LVHW100345251120
672555LV00014B/293